■SCHOLASTIC

Easy Reader Biographies™

Teaching Guide

Strategies • Mini-Lessons • Graphic Organizers

by Pamela Chanko

NEW YORK • TORONTO • LONDON • AUCKLAND • SYDNEY
MEXICO CITY • NEW DELHI • HONG KONG • BUENOS AIRES

Teaching Resources

Teaching guide written by Pamela Chanko

Cover design by Maria Lilja

Cover illustrations by Renee Graef

Interior illustrations by Cheryl Phelps

Interior design by Sydney Wright

ISBN: 978-0-439-77412-3

Copyright © 2007 by Scholastic Inc.

Published by Scholastic Inc.

All rights reserved.

Printed in China.

16   15   14   13   12   11   62   18   17   16   15   14

Contents

Introduction 5

How to Use the Program 6

Connections to the Standards 8

Guided Reading and Nonfiction Feature Grid 10

Sample Guided Reading Lesson 12

Teaching Nonfiction Text 14

Teaching the Biographies 18

Using the Graphic Organizers 19

Graphic Organizers to Use With Any Book:

    Sequencing Timeline 20

    Vocabulary Chart 21

    Character Map 22

    Venn Diagram 23

Book-by-Book Teaching Pages and Reproducibles

Susan B. Anthony: Fighter for Women's Rights

    Teaching Page 24

    Reproducible 25

Johnny Appleseed: An American Who Made a Difference

    Teaching Page 26

    Reproducible 27

Alexander Graham Bell: A Famous Inventor

    Teaching Page 28

    Reproducible 29

Cesar Chavez: A Leader for Change

    Teaching Page 30

    Reproducible 31

Helen Keller: An Inspiring Life

    Teaching Page 32

    Reproducible 33

Martin Luther King, Jr.: A Man With a Dream

Teaching Page 34

Reproducible 35

Abraham Lincoln: A Great President, a Great American

Teaching Page 36

Reproducible 37

Rosa Parks: Bus Ride to Freedom

Teaching Page 38

Reproducible 39

Betsy Ross: The Story of Our Flag

Teaching Page 40

Reproducible 41

Squanto: A Friend to the Pilgrims

Teaching Page 42

Reproducible 43

Harriet Tubman: Follow the North Star

Teaching Page 44

Reproducible 45

George Washington: America's First President

Teaching Page 46

Reproducible 47

Selected References 48

Introduction

Everyone loves a good story—and when that story is true, it can be even more compelling. Teaching history is an essential part of any curriculum, but children are more likely to absorb (and enjoy!) what they learn about their country's past when it is told through narrative, rather than when it is presented as rote facts and dates. And that's what *Easy Reader Biographies* is all about— riveting stories! We've chosen 12 remarkable people who have faced challenges, followed dreams, and fought for causes, helping to shape our country's identity as well as their own. From Johnny Appleseed's cross-country mission to Harriet Tubman's brave journey to freedom, the lives of these amazing people are sure to inspire children.

In addition, the program is designed to make nonfiction accessible and engaging. As teachers, we need to prepare even the youngest learners for increasing academic demands, and give them the skills they need to interpret nonfiction material both in and out of school. *Easy Reader Biographies* introduces children to nonfiction features such as picture captions and glossaries, as well as easy-to-read graphics such as timelines, diagrams, and maps—all within the context of exciting, true-life stories.

Perhaps most important of all, *Easy Reader Biographies* is a flexible, easy-to-use program designed to meet your teaching needs. The helpful features you'll find in the program include:

- a handy storage box designed to create an inviting book display
- five copies of each book, allowing for both independent reading and group instruction
- teaching pages with step-by-step strategies for each title
- an engaging reproducible graphic organizer for each title, designed to boost comprehension and critical thinking skills

  . . . and much more!

With *Easy Reader Biographies*, children will develop essential reading skills, build core content knowledge and cultural literacy, and meet some amazing Americans who are sure to inspire.

How to Use the Program

Easy Reader Biographies is a nonfiction reading program designed to support and enhance any curriculum. The books can be used in a variety of ways to meet the needs of your students. In addition, this teaching guide provides a wealth of strategies and tips to help you maximize children's learning. Use the following options to guide you in tailoring the program to your curriculum.

Setting Up the Books

The handy storage box can be used to create an inviting book display. Remove the lid and hang it on the back of the box; then place the box on a countertop at students' eye level. Inside the box, you'll find five copies of each of the 12 titles. The tiered shelves are designed to display six titles at a time, two in each row. Rotate your display as needed to feature different titles.

Using the Teacher's Guide

This complete teaching resource provides you with all the materials you'll need to get the most out of the program in your classroom. In this guide, you'll find the following:

• A rationale for making the program part of your reading, writing, and social studies curriculum. **Connections to the Standards** (pages 8–9) presents each important standard your students will meet through reading the books as well as through the lessons and activities featured in this teaching guide.

• A **Guided Reading and Nonfiction Feature Grid** (pages 10–11) that shows each book's guided reading level, word count, vocabulary, and nonfiction features at a glance.

• A **Sample Guided Reading Lesson** (pages 12–13) to use as a model for teaching the texts with guided reading groups.

• **Teaching Nonfiction Text** (pages 14–17), which provides research and strategies to help children learn how to read and comprehend key features of nonfiction.

• **Teaching the Biographies** (page 18), which provides a guide for presenting the books to children, including suggestions for before, during, and after reading.

• Four **Graphic Organizers to Use With Any Book** (pages 20–23), easy-to-use reproducibles that reinforce children's learning and build critical skills.

• One **Teaching Page** and one **Reproducible** for each title in the program (pages 24–47). The titles are organized in alphabetical order. You might present the stories in chronological order or choose books that coincide with a particular topic of study or holiday, such as Presidents' Day or Martin Luther King, Jr., Day. On these pages, you'll find:

- A short synopsis with background information about the biography's subject.
- Strategies, questions, and discussion ideas to introduce the book to children.
- A step-by-step guide for teaching the spotlighted nonfiction feature.
- Simple instructions for using the reproducible after reading.
- A short list of book links—titles to check out if children would like to learn more.
- After-reading reproducibles—each title's activity sheet focuses on essential comprehension skills, such as cause and effect, comparison and contrast, sequencing, and personal reading response.

Using the Books to Teach Nonfiction Text

The biographies in this program provide a great venue for teaching the genre of nonfiction. Embedded in each book are a variety of nonfiction text structures, such as chronological order, cause and effect, and problem and solution. Every book contains the essential nonfiction features of realistic illustrations, captions, bold-faced words, and a glossary. In addition, each title has one or two spotlighted nonfiction features—these include maps, diagrams, bulleted lists, timelines, and more.

Using the Books for Independent Reading

These biographies make perfect additions to your independent reading library. You can display the books in the provided storage box, or if you prefer, place them in a basket labeled "Biographies." Invite children to browse through the books and choose one to read during independent reading time. Or place one of the titles in a resealable bag for each student, along with other books at his or her reading level.

Using the Books for Guided Reading

These books are also excellent choices for guided reading. Each book correlates with guided reading level I or J. (See the grid on pages 10–11 for leveling information about each title.) This will help you select titles at just the right level for each student. Research shows that books are "just right" when children are able to read and understand the majority of the text and are able to use strategies to figure out most of the unknown words they encounter. The teacher is then able to provide scaffolding, assisting with challenging concepts and providing prompts to boost comprehension and build self-correction strategies.

   Since five copies of each title are included, you can easily group students and use one title for small-group instruction. On pages 12–13, you'll find a sample guided reading lesson to use with *Rosa Parks: Bus Ride to Freedom*. Use the sample as a model to plan guided reading lessons for the other titles in the program. The grid on pages 10–11 allows you to preview each title's reading level, word count, average number of words per page, and vocabulary, so you can tailor your instruction to meet students' needs.

Connections to the Standards

The books and lessons in this program are designed to support you in meeting the following standards for students in grades K–2, outlined by Mid-continent Research for Education and Learning (McREL), an organization that collects and synthesizes national and state K–12 curriculum standards.

Civics

- Understands ideas about civic life, politics, and government.

- Understands the essential characteristics of limited and unlimited governments.

- Understands the sources, purposes, and functions of law, and the importance of the rule of law for the protection of individual rights and the common good.

- Understands the central ideas of American constitutional government and how this form of government has shaped the character of American society.

- Understands issues regarding personal, political, and economic rights.

- Understands issues regarding the proper scope and limits of rights and the relationships among personal, political, and economic rights.

- Understands how certain character traits enhance citizens' ability to fulfill personal and civic responsibilities.

- Understands the importance of political leadership, public service, and a knowledgeable citizenry in American constitutional democracy.

Geography

- Understands the characteristics and uses of maps and other geographic tools.

- Knows the location of places and geographic features.

- Understands the physical and human characteristics of place.

- Understands how geography is used to interpret the past.

History

- Understands the causes and nature of movements of large groups of people into and within the United States.

- Understands major discoveries in science and technology, some of their social and economic effects, and the major scientists and inventors responsible for them.

- Understands how communities in North America varied long ago, including:
    - Understands changes in community life over time.
    - Understands the contributions and significance of historical figures of the community.

- Understands how democratic values came to be, and how they have been exemplified by people, events, and symbols, including:
  - Knows the English colonists who became revolutionary leaders and fought for independence from England, such as George Washington and Thomas Jefferson.
  - Understands how individuals have worked to achieve the liberties and equality promised in the principles of American democracy and to improve the lives of people from many groups, such as Rosa Parks, Martin Luther King, Jr., and Cesar Chavez.
  - Understands how important figures reacted to their times and why they were significant to the history of our democracy, such as George Washington, Thomas Jefferson, Abraham Lincoln, Susan B. Anthony, and Martin Luther King, Jr.
  - Understands the ways in which people in a variety of fields have advanced the cause of human rights, equality, and the common good, such as Rosa Parks and Cesar Chavez.
  - Understands the reasons that Americans celebrate certain national holidays.
  - Knows the history of American symbols.
  - Knows why important buildings, statues, and monuments are associated with state and national history.
  - Understands how people have helped newcomers get settled and learn the ways of the new country.

Historical Understanding

- Understands and knows how to analyze chronological relationships and patterns.

Language Arts

- Uses the general skills and strategies of the writing process.
- Uses the stylistic and rhetorical aspects of writing.
- Uses grammatical and mechanical conventions in written compositions.
- Uses the general skills and strategies of the reading process, including:
  - Uses meaning clues such as picture captions, title, cover, and headings to aid comprehension.
- Uses reading skills and strategies to understand and interpret a variety of informational texts, including:
  - Understands the main idea and supporting details of simple expository information.
  - Relates new information to prior knowledge and experience.

Source: *Content Knowledge: A Compendium of Standards and Benchmarks for K–12 Education.* 4th edition (Mid-continent Research for Education and Learning, 2004).

Guided Reading and Nonfiction Feature Grid

Title	SUSAN B. ANTHONY: Fighter for Women's Rights	JOHNNY APPLESEED: An American Who Made a Difference	ALEXANDER GRAHAM BELL: A Famous Inventor	CESAR CHAVEZ: A Leader for Change	HELEN KELLER: An Inspiring Life	MARTIN LUTHER KING, JR.: A Man With a Dream
Guided Reading Level	J	I	I	I	J	I
Word Count	665	638	631	707	666	707
Average Number of Words per Page	42	40	39	44	42	44
Vocabulary	arrested convention election equal passionate property rights timeline	herb medicine orchard settler snowshoe trudged wilderness	deaf fascinated incredible inventor laboratory tube vibration wire	boycott crop migrant farmworker register strike union	Braille communicate hope inspiring palm realized timeline	boycott equal law mourned pastor protest segregation
General Nonfiction Features	realistic illustrations, captions, glossary	realistic illustrations, captions, glossary	realistic illustrations, captions, glossary	realistic illustrations, captions, glossary	realistic illustrations, captions, glossary	realistic illustrations, captions, glossary
Spotlight Nonfiction Features	list timeline	diagram flowchart map	diagram	list	timeline	illustrated examples with captions

ABRAHAM LINCOLN: A Great President, a Great American	ROSA PARKS: Bus Ride to Freedom	BETSY ROSS: The Story of Our Flag	SQUANTO: A Friend to the Pilgrims	HARRIET TUBMAN: Follow the North Star	GEORGE WASHINGTON: America's First President
I	J	I	I	I	J
631	826	649	584	700	692
39	52	41	37	44	43

Civil War
lawyer
master
president
slave
trustworthy
	arrested
	boycott
	civil rights
	equally
	segregate
	Supreme
	  Court
	trial
		chore
		colony
		official
		sketch
		supplies
		upholsterer
			celebration
			crop
			explorer
			harvest
			settler
			slave
			trader
			Wampanoag
				capture
				Civil War
				conductor
				escaped
				master
				slave
				Underground
				  Railroad
					colony
					elected
					inspired
					manners
					monument
					trade
					uniform

realistic illustrations, captions, glossary	realistic illustrations, captions, glossary	realistic illustrations, captions, glossary	realistic illustrations, captions, glossary	realistic illustrations, captions, glossary	realistic illustrations, captions, glossary
map	timeline	diagram	diagram	map	list diagram

Sample Guided Reading Lesson

Rosa Parks: Bus Ride to Freedom

First Reading

Routine	Sample
Teacher Preview • Read the book to preview content and vocabulary. • Scan for both supportive and challenging text features.	**Summary:** *Rosa Parks: Bus Ride to Freedom* tells the story of Parks's life. The book focuses on the story of her famous bus ride, which catapulted the civil rights movement. **Supportive Features:** The story is told in sequential order, and each page has a limited line count. The illustrations help clarify meaning in both the main text and captions. **Challenging Features:** Children may need help defining broad concepts such as civil rights. Build background on the concept of equal treatment by providing examples familiar to children, such as fairness at school. In addition, some children may need help reading the dialogue in quotation marks on page 8.
Introduce the Book • Display and discuss the cover. Read the title and the names of the author and illustrator. • Take a picture walk through the book and have children predict events.	▪ Invite children to examine the book's cover. Read the title, as well as the author's and illustrator's names. ▪ Explain to children that this book will teach them about the life of Rosa Parks, a real person in history. Point out the illustration of Parks on the cover. You might show students a photograph of Rosa Parks to emphasize this point. ▪ Invite children to preview the pictures, using what they know about the title to make predictions about Parks's story. Ask: ▸ How old does Rosa look at the beginning of the book? At the end? ▸ What do you think happened on the bus?
Pre-Teach Vocabulary • Introduce the bold-faced vocabulary words, using the glossary and illustrations where applicable.	▪ Have children turn to the glossary on page 16. Have them point to each word as you read it aloud and then echo-read the word after you. ▪ Read the definition of each word and discuss its meaning. Use each word in a sentence, and show a supportive illustration if there is one. ▪ Use prompts like these to help children think about the new words: ▸ Finish this sentence: *If people break the law, they might get _____.* ▸ Which word means almost the same as *separated*?
Read the Book • Guide children as they read the book. • Help with decoding as children come upon difficult words. • Check comprehension as children read.	▪ Have children read to themselves softly, one or two pages at a time. ▪ Listen in to each member of the group. As difficult words come up, assist with decoding. ▪ You may want to stop children's reading periodically and ask questions to monitor comprehension. Questions might include: **Page 1:** Who is this story mostly about? **Page 3:** What can you tell about Rosa's school from the picture? **Page 7:** Why does the driver tell Rosa to move? What does the caption tell you? **Page 11:** In what way did the rules on the bus change? **Page 13:** Does this picture show a bus from today, or long ago? How can you tell?

Revisit and Reinforce

Routine	Sample
Teach a Comprehension Strategy • Choose a specific comprehension strategy to model and teach. • Have children use a graphic organizer to practice the skill.	**Sequencing** • Explain to children that biographies are often told in chronological, or time, order. Learning the events in the order they happened can help children understand how one event may have led to the next. Use prompts such as: ▸ What was the first thing Rosa did to fight for civil rights? ▸ What happened on December 1, 1955? ▸ What happened after Rosa did not give up her seat on the bus? ▸ When did people decide to boycott the bus? ▸ Look at the timeline on pages 14–15 of the book. How does it show the sequence of events? • Distribute copies of the Sequencing Timeline on page 20 of this guide. Have children fill it in to show the most important events of Parks's life in order.
Teach Phonics • Select a phonics skill and choose decodable words from the book to reinforce the skill. • Lead blending and word-building activities with these words.	**Long Vowels With Final *e*** • Write the following words from the book on the board: *time, white, five, rode, like, home, came, side, ride, spoke.* • Review with children that in these words the final *e* gives the vowel a long sound. Have children say the long-*i* sound. Then model how to blend the word *five.* Ask: *What other words have the long-i sound?* • Repeat the procedure for other long-*i* words, as well as long-*o* and long-*a* words. • Begin a long-vowel word-building chart on the board. Head columns with these word families: *-ide, -ake, -oke.* Help children add initial consonants, blends, and digraphs to build words.
Writing Option • Choose one or two writing activities to assess comprehension and extend learning.	**Check Understanding** • Write a letter to the bus company explaining why the rules for African Americans were unfair. **Extend Learning** • Write a journal entry telling about a time when you were treated unfairly, and what you did about it.
Building Fluency • Model one or more aspects of fluency, such as pace, tone, or expression. • Help children build fluency with repeated reading activities.	**Model Tone and Dialogue** • Read aloud pages 6–8 in the book. Tell children that you will use a special voice for dialogue (the words people say out loud), so that listeners will know who is speaking. Have children echo-read after you, matching your tone, pace, and expression. **Repeated Reading: Readers Theater** • Pair children, having one child read Rosa Parks's part of the dialogue and the other child read the bus driver's part. Have both children read the narration chorally.

Teaching Nonfiction Text

Why Teach Nonfiction?

For some time, it was widely believed that children naturally preferred fictional storybooks over any other genre, including informational and nonfiction text. However, recent research has indicated otherwise. When analyzing the books that first-grade students self-selected for independent reading time, the researchers found that many actually preferred nonfiction (Donovan, Smolkin, and Lomax, 2000; Caswell and Duke, 1998, as cited in Boyton and Blevins, 2004).

Does this mean that nonfiction should be made the focus of all early-elementary reading programs? Of course not. But it does indicate that a healthy balance of fiction and nonfiction is key. The *Easy Reader Biographies* program helps you strike this balance by "bridging the gap" between fiction and nonfiction. Children who naturally gravitate toward informational text will get plenty of the content knowledge they crave. And children who *do* prefer stories will get engaging narratives, making these books a perfect introduction to the nonfiction genre.

What the Research Says

Research has provided insight into the importance of teaching nonfiction. Here are some key findings:

- Many students struggle with content area reading (Vacca, 2002; Walpole, 1998, as cited in Kristo and Bamford, 2004). Providing students with high-quality nonfiction materials may help to better prepare them to meet these challenges.

- Providing students in the younger grades with more exposure to nonfiction may alleviate the decline in achievement often observed in fourth grade (Chall, Jacobs, and Baldwin, 1990; Duke, 2000, as cited in Boyton and Blevins, 2005).

- The reading materials students encounter influence their writing (Tierney and Shanahan, 1996, as cited in Kristo and Bamford, 2004). In order to prepare students to write nonfiction, it's important to teach them how to read nonfiction texts and to provide them with many opportunities to practice reading these materials.

- Exposing students in the early grades to informational texts helps improve their skills as readers and writers of informational text when they are older (Papps, 1991; Sanacore, 1991, as cited in Kirsto and Bamford, 2004).

The Benefits of Teaching Nonfiction

While we all know that we can help children develop great reading habits by catering to their natural interests, it's essential to think about the specific skills children will be getting from their reading material as well. Here are just some of the benefits of teaching nonfiction in the classroom.

It builds vocabulary. Nonfiction text and informational text expose children to vocabulary they will most likely not encounter in storybooks or in everyday conversation. Each content area has its own specialized language, and history text is no different. The books in this program will familiarize children with such terms as *settler, trader, colony, convention, election,* and many more. With challenging vocabulary comes challenging concepts, and the biographies help children grasp these as well. For instance, what is *equality*? What does it mean to fight for *civil rights*? When these concepts are introduced in context, they become more concrete. Plus, studies have shown that children who hear nonfiction read aloud on a regular basis begin to incorporate its special language into their own vocabulary over time.

It increases content knowledge. Children learn a great deal about the world around them through their own experience. Teachers can supplement that experience by giving children world knowledge they will not encounter on their own. To truly absorb this content, children must learn how to connect their prior, or personal, knowledge to unfamiliar information. By teaching historical content through a personal perspective, the books in this program help children gain an understanding of such events and concepts as the Civil War, the Underground Railroad, the suffrage movement, and more.

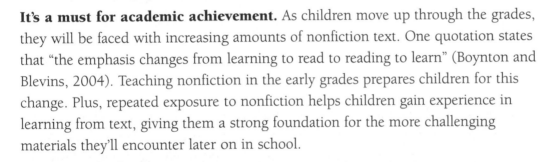

It's a must for academic achievement. As children move up through the grades, they will be faced with increasing amounts of nonfiction text. One quotation states that "the emphasis changes from learning to read to reading to learn" (Boynton and Blevins, 2004). Teaching nonfiction in the early grades prepares children for this change. Plus, repeated exposure to nonfiction helps children gain experience in learning from text, giving them a strong foundation for the more challenging materials they'll encounter later on in school.

It's essential for successful test taking. The emphasis on standardized testing is a challenge for both teachers and students. Children must learn to navigate both narratives and informational texts in order to be successful. Providing direct instruction with nonfiction text increases children's comprehension of the genre, a necessary skill for achieving and maintaining good test scores.

Teaching Nonfiction Features With the Program

We've established that teaching nonfiction is of vital importance—so the question that naturally follows is "How do we teach it?" Nonfiction can be challenging because it has unique features that differentiate it from fiction. Children need direct instruction in navigating these features, and the *Easy Reader Biographies* program is specifically designed to help you provide it.

When reading storybooks, children usually need only to follow the flow of text from left to right and top to bottom. However, much of nonfiction contains additional features that interrupt the flow of text, such as pictures with captions, diagrams and labels, maps, charts, and bulleted lists. Children must learn to navigate the page in order to gain a deeper understanding of the information. Following are features you'll find throughout the program, along with strategies for direct instruction.

Nonfiction Features in Every Book

Each of the 12 titles in the program contains these basic nonfiction elements.

Realistic Illustrations With Captions Realistic illustrations are vital to nonfiction—particularly historical text—because they help children form a picture of the people and events being described. On every page, above the main text, you'll find an illustration that supports the information given. Many of the illustrations include captions. Each caption is tied to both the information in the main text and the information visually presented in the illustration. Encourage children to read the main text first. Next, they should take a brief look at the illustration. Then, have them read the caption before examining the illustration again, looking for visual details. If they prefer, children may read the main text one more time to tie it all together.

Bold-faced Words Throughout the books, challenging or specialized vocabulary is printed in boldface. Explain to children that when they encounter a bold-faced word, they should pay particular attention to it. The dark type not only indicates that the word may be difficult but also that it's an important word—children need to understand what it means in order to grasp the information. Let children know that they can find definitions for these words in the glossary on page 16.

Glossary Each bold-faced word also appears in the glossary on the last page of every book. Explain to children that a glossary is like a mini-dictionary. It gives the meaning of important and/or unfamiliar words in the text. Children can preview the glossary before they read to see what special words they will encounter. Then, as they read, they can look up bold-faced words as needed by turning to the back page.

Spotlighted Nonfiction Features

Each title also contains one or two "spotlight" features, allowing you to focus on different features with each title.

Map In addition to showing where places are located, maps can provide all kinds of information. A transportation map can show a route, or how people get from one place to another. A map can also show political information, such as boundaries between states or countries. Physical maps show features such as mountains and rivers. Historical maps can give perspective by showing how a place has changed over time. Tell children that it's important to read the map's title or caption first. This will tell them what information the map shows. If the map has symbols or is color coded, children should read the caption or key to see what the colors and symbols mean. Finally, have them read any labels, such as names of places.

Timeline Timelines show dates and give a brief description of events in chronological order. Since timelines often cover a broad span of years, they provide historical perspective, helping the reader see a whole time period at a glance. Have children read the timeline's title or caption first to see what events will be covered. Next, children should look at the first and last dates to see how long a period the timeline represents. Finally, have children read each date and event in sequential order from left to right. To analyze the timeline, ask children which events took place before or after other events. To encourage critical thinking, challenge children to look at the order of events and think about how one may have led to the next.

Diagram Diagrams help readers see parts of a whole or show how something works. The illustration is usually detailed and has labels to name its different parts. Like any other nonfiction feature, children should read the diagram's title or caption first to see what the picture will explain. Next, they should look at the picture as a whole to get a general idea of what's being presented. Finally, have children read each label. If the labels have arrows, show children how to trace the arrow's path to the correct part of the picture.

Flowchart A flowchart is a special kind of diagram that shows steps in a process. The chart contains a series of pictures that are often numbered and connected by arrows. The main title or caption tells children what process the flowchart shows. After reading the title, children should look at each picture in numerical order, reading additional captions if they are present. Children can also use the arrows to see how each step in the process leads to the next.

List Lists provide lots of information in a small space. They're a valuable nonfiction feature because the text is chunked, clearly separating each idea from the rest. In this way, each fact stands out and can therefore be more easily remembered. Explain to children that bulleted lists contain related facts—each fact on the list relates to, or is an example of, the main idea or topic. Lists begin with a sentence or part of a sentence that tells the main idea. Children should always read the list's introduction first, so they can see how the items in the list tie together. As they read each subsequent item, encourage them to think about how it relates to the main idea.

Illustrated Examples With Captions This special text feature is closely related to the list described above. However, it gives the information an added visual element. Usually, one main caption appears above the group of illustrations. This serves the same purpose as a list's introduction—it gives the main idea. Illustrated examples follow, each with its own mini-caption. Be sure children read the main caption first. Then have them read each mini-caption, looking at the illustration for details.

Teaching the Biographies

For each title in the program, you'll find a correlated teaching page with specific strategies to use for that book as well as a reproducible to use after reading (see pages 24–47). Following are some general tips and strategies for using the books with students.

Before Reading

Prepare children for reading the book with these strategies.

* Activate prior knowledge about the subject by tapping into children's related personal experiences and background knowledge. In addition, invite children who have heard of the person to share what they already know.

* Build background about the time and place in which the person lived. Preview the text before sharing it with children, and provide them with a few key points.

* Introduce the glossary words and discuss the meanings of each. For younger children, you might introduce a few words at a time and then revisit the words at a later time.

* Preview the title and cover together. Have children describe what the person looks like and tell what the title says about him or her.

* Take a picture walk through the book, inviting children to make predictions about events from the illustrations.

During Reading

Boost comprehension during reading with these suggestions.

* When children come upon an unfamiliar word in boldface, encourage them to look it up in the glossary. If the word is not bold-faced, help them use any context clues to guess its meaning. Keep a children's dictionary nearby to use as necessary.

* Help children follow the chronological order by pausing periodically and having them sequence the events so far using their own words.

* Assess comprehension as you read by providing prompts and questions. In addition to recall questions (*Where did Harriet Tubman grow up?*), give children prompts that require critical thinking (*Why did Harriet run away from the plantation? What does this tell you about her?*).

After Reading

Help children retain and extend their learning with these ideas.

* Hold a group discussion, inviting children to share their personal reactions. How do they feel about the person they just read about, and why?

* Give children a writing prompt. You might have them write a letter to the person, or write what they themselves might have done in that person's situation. Younger children can dictate their response.

* Have children work in small groups to dramatize the person's life story. Assign each child a role and invite groups to use improvised actions and dialogue to act out an important event or pivotal scene.

Using the Graphic Organizers

Graphic organizers are an effective way to enhance children's comprehension and critical thinking skills, in addition to building their confidence as emergent writers. Following each teaching page, you'll find a reproducible graphic organizer to use as a reading response activity for that particular biography. On pages 20–23, you'll find general graphic organizers to use with any of the biographies. They are easily adaptable to any skill level: Children can complete them using dictation, drawing, writing on their own, or working with a partner.

Sequencing Timeline

Sequencing is an important comprehension skill, especially when reading biographies. Usually, the story of a person's life is told in chronological order, leading readers to see how one event led to the next. Invite children to use the timeline on page 20 to record and analyze important events in each famous American's life. Have children page through the book, noting pivotal events in the person's story. They can create their own timeline by filling in the boxes with information about the events. Have children write the events in order, from left to right. If desired, have them include the dates of events when provided in the text.

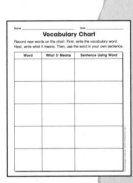

Vocabulary Chart

The books in this program are designed to build vocabulary by incorporating challenging words and concepts into easy-to-read text. Have children use the chart on page 21 to keep track of their new words. In the first column, have children write the word. Next, have them look up the word's meaning, either in the glossary or in a dictionary. In the second column, have them write the word's definition. In the last column, have children write their own sentence using the word in context.

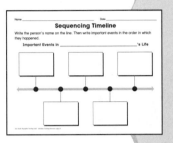

Character Map

Children can use the character map on page 22 to analyze and synthesize ideas about each biographical subject. In the center, have children write the famous American's name. In the surrounding boxes, children can write important events that shaped the person's life, their major accomplishments, their character traits, and how they feel about him or her.

Venn Diagram

Use the Venn diagram on page 23 to help children compare two people they've read about. Have them label the circles with each person's name and then write facts about each person in the corresponding circle. In the center, have children write what the two people had in common. For instance, Susan B. Anthony was a leader in the suffrage movement, while Rosa Parks played an important role in the civil rights movement. Both women stood up against unfair treatment, and both were willing to get arrested in the fight for their cause.

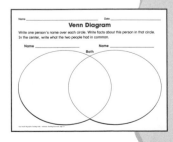

Sequencing Timeline

Write the person's name on the line. Then write important events in the order in which they happened.

Important Events in _____'s Life

Name _____   Date _____

Vocabulary Chart

Record new words on the chart. First, write the vocabulary word.
Next, write what it means. Then, use the word in your own sentence.

Word	What It Means	Sentence Using Word

Name _____

Date _____

Character Map

Write the person's name in the center box. Then fill in the other boxes.

His or Her Accomplishments:

Important Events in the Person's Life:

Name:

How I Feel About the Person:

What the Person Was Like:

Name _____

Date _____

Venn Diagram

Write one person's name over each circle. Write facts about this person in that circle. In the center, write what the two people had in common.

Name _____

Name _____

Both

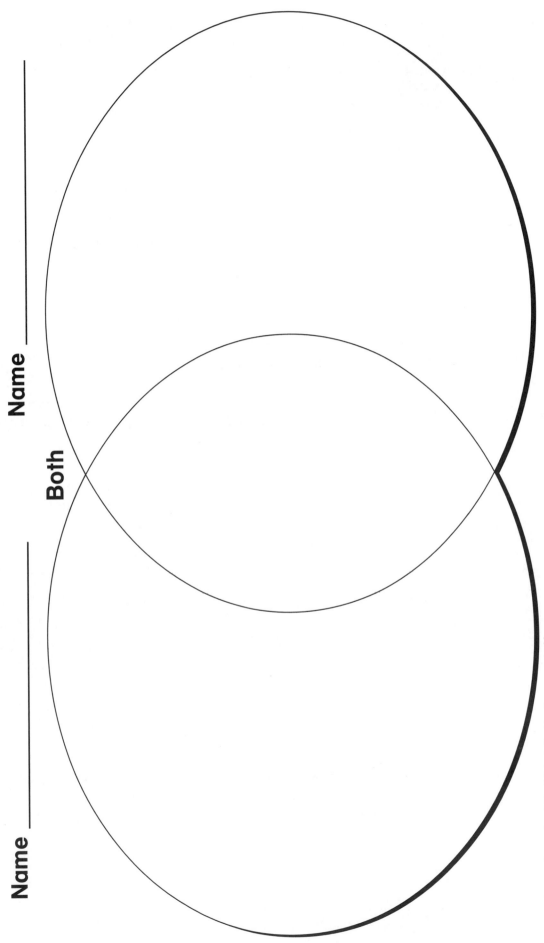

Susan B. Anthony
Fighter for Women's Rights

Susan B. Anthony lived from 1820 to 1906, when many basic rights were not extended to women. They could not own property, they were excluded from most jobs, and they could not vote. Anthony worked for more than 50 years as an activist for equal rights. She did not live to see women win the right to vote—but her brave determination paved the way for change.

Guided Reading Level: J

Word Count: 665

Average Words Per Page: 42

Spotlight Nonfiction Feature:
List, Timeline

Introducing the Book

Introduce the concept of suffrage with a class vote, such as what book to read. Tally the votes. Then ask children to imagine how they would feel if only certain children were allowed to vote, such as children who are wearing red that day. Ask: *Is this fair?* Tell children that you will honor the whole-group decision, but there was a time when decisions were not made so fairly. Women and men were not treated equally, and only men could vote. Today they will read about a woman who helped change these laws.

Spotlight Nonfiction Features: List and Timeline

Explain that nonfiction text often presents a lot of information and uses different formats to do this. Special features, such as lists and timelines, help readers see this information quickly and easily.

First, have children turn to the list on page 5. Point out that the text is broken into small chunks with marks called *bullets*. Each bullet presents a different fact. Then direct children to the list's heading, which tells the main idea, or what the facts are all about. Ask: *Is the order of sentences on the list important? Why or why not?* (No, the order is not important. The sentences are all details that relate to the main idea.)

Next, turn to the timeline on pages 14–15.

Point out that this feature has chunked text as well—each point presents one event. Help children understand the purpose of the timeline by asking: *Is the order of events on the timeline important?* (Yes, the events are shown in the order in which they happened.)

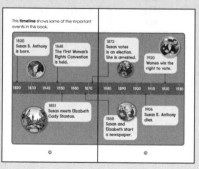

Using the Reproducible

Give children copies of page 25 and invite them to choose a current female hero. It can be someone they know or a famous woman they admire. Have children list her accomplishments. Then ask: *Could your hero have done these things before Anthony's time? How did the fight for equal rights help your hero get where she is today?*

Book Links

For more information on Susan B. Anthony and the suffrage movement, try these titles:

- *The Ballot Box Battle* by Emily Arnold McCully (Random House, 1996)
- *I Could Do That! Esther Morris Gets Women the Vote* by Linda Arms White (Farrar, Straus and Giroux, 2005)
- *Susan B. Anthony* by Lucile Davis (Capstone, 1998)

Award of Honor

Choose a woman you admire who is living today. Write her name and what she has done. Then write how Susan B. Anthony's fight for equality helped your hero.

My Hero	
Name	
Accomplishments	
How Susan B. Anthony Helped My Hero	

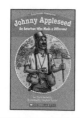

Johnny Appleseed
An American Who Made a Difference

John Chapman (1774–1845) is known as "Johnny Appleseed" for his famous cross-country mission: populating the Midwest with apple trees for the pioneers to enjoy. A lover of nature and a friend to the environment, Johnny Appleseed traveled the country for nearly 50 years, planting apple seeds along the way. Some say we are still enjoying the fruits of his labor today!

Guided Reading Level: I

Word Count: 638

Average Words Per Page: 40

Spotlight Nonfiction Feature: Flowchart, Map

Introducing the Book

Invite children to share prior knowledge about apples. Ask: *What are some ways to eat apples? Have you ever had apple juice, apple pie, or applesauce?* Point out that apples are one of the most popular fruits in our country. Then ask: *Have you ever seen an apple tree? Where do you think the trees come from?*

Slice up an apple and share it with the group. Point out the apple seeds. Tell children they will be reading about a man who got his nickname from apple seeds.

Spotlight Nonfiction Features: Chart and Map

Have children turn to page 7, directing them to the numbered pictures at the top of the page. Explain that a flowchart is a series of pictures that shows the steps in a process. It helps readers visualize the order in which something happens. Read the heading aloud. Then point out the numbers and arrows and explain that they show the order of steps. Invite children to study each picture in order, describing in their own words what happens first, second, third, and fourth.

Next, turn to the map on pages 12–13. Explain that a map is like a flat picture of Earth. It is a view from above of the land. Maps can show all kinds of information, from where things are to what plants grow in different areas. First, read the caption and explain that this tells what the map shows. Next, point out the symbols. Ask: *What do you think the apples and trees stand for?* (They stand for the route along which Johnny Appleseed planted apple seeds.) *What do the arrows show?* (They show the direction in which he traveled.) Have children read the name of each state along Johnny's route.

Using the Reproducible

Discuss how Johnny Appleseed was a friend to Earth by helping plants, animals, and people. Give children copies of page 27 and have them write in each apple one way Johnny helped Earth. (He planted trees; he grew food for settlers; he was kind to animals.) In the trunk, have children write one thing they could do to help Earth.

Book Links

For more information on Johnny Appleseed, try these titles:

◆ *Johnny Appleseed* by Patricia Brennan Demuth (Penguin, 1996)

◆ *Johnny Appleseed: My Story* by David Lee Harrison (Random House, 2001)

◆ *The Story of Johnny Appleseed* by Aliki (Simon & Schuster, 1963)

Johnny Appleseed's Tree

Johnny was a friend to Earth. He made a difference to plants, animals, and people. In each apple, write one thing Johnny did for our planet. On the trunk, write one thing you can do for Earth.

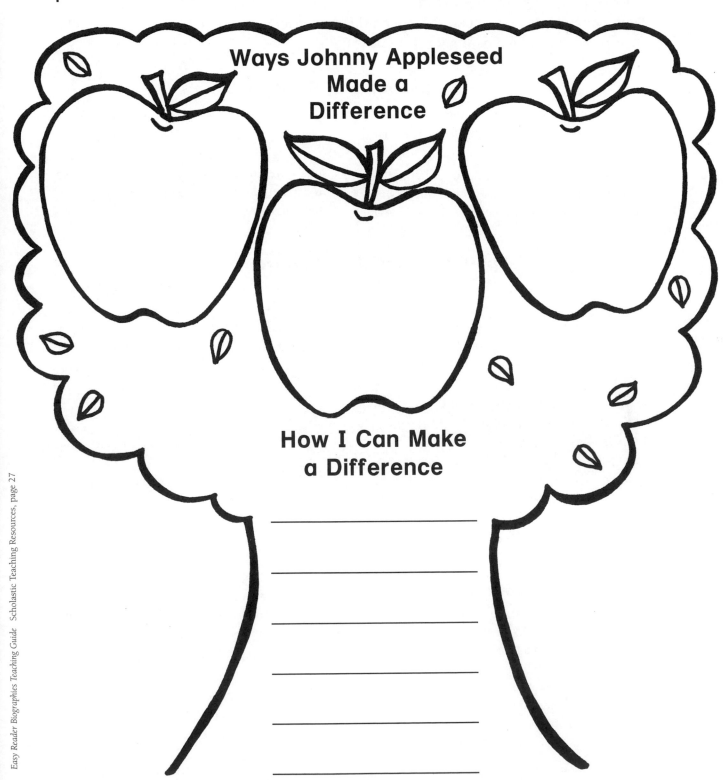

Ways Johnny Appleseed Made a Difference

How I Can Make a Difference

Alexander Graham Bell
A Famous Inventor

Guided Reading Level: I

Word Count: 631

Average Words Per Page: 39

Spotlight Nonfiction Feature: Diagram

Alexander Graham Bell (1847–1922) was an innovator who changed American life forever. Always fascinated by sound, he began his career as a teacher of deaf children. Then he began working full-time on his inventions—and in 1876, he invented the telephone. Throughout his life, Bell continued to work on different inventions and he continued to find ways to help deaf people.

Introducing the Book

Activate prior knowledge by asking: *When was the last time you talked to someone on the phone? Who was it, and how far does this person live from you?*

Encourage children to imagine what life was like before the telephone. Ask: *If you wanted to invite a friend over who lived across town, how would you do it?* (You might go in person or send a note.) *How would you stay in touch with a relative who lived far away?* (You would write letters.) Lead children to see the important role the telephone plays in their daily lives. Then explain that they'll be reading about the man who invented it.

Spotlight Nonfiction Feature: Diagram

Talk with children about the purpose of diagrams. Explain that diagrams are pictures that show parts of something, or how a machine or a process works. Then explain that some diagrams show how something (such as an invention) has changed over time.

Have children turn to page 15. Explain that the caption tells what information the diagram shows, and ask a volunteer to read it aloud. Next, point out the year labels connected to each telephone. Ask: *How is the diagram helpful? Why might it be better than a written description of each year's phone?* (It helps readers visualize the phones; it gives a lot of information in a small space.)

Use the diagram for a mini telephone quiz. Ask: *How did the telephone change from 1876 to 1919? What's the biggest difference between the 1964 phone and the 1992 phone? Do you think the phone has improved between 1876 and today? How?*

Alexander worked hard to make people's lives better. People will always think of the telephone as his greatest invention. The next time you call someone, remember Alexander Graham Bell.

Using the Reproducible

Give children copies of the graphic organizer on page 29. Explain that the biography they just read describes how Alexander Graham Bell invented the telephone, but it also tells several other things about his life. Invite children to write four other things they learned about Bell.

Book Links

For more information on Alexander Graham Bell and the telephone, try these titles:

- *Alexander Graham Bell* by Victoria Sherrow (Lerner, 2003)
- *Alexander Graham Bell: An Inventive Life* by Elizabeth MacLeod (Kids Can Press, 1999)
- *The Telephone* by Marc Tyler Nobleman (Capstone, 2004)

All About Bell

Alexander Graham Bell is best known for inventing the telephone. What else did you learn about him? In each phone, write a detail from the book.

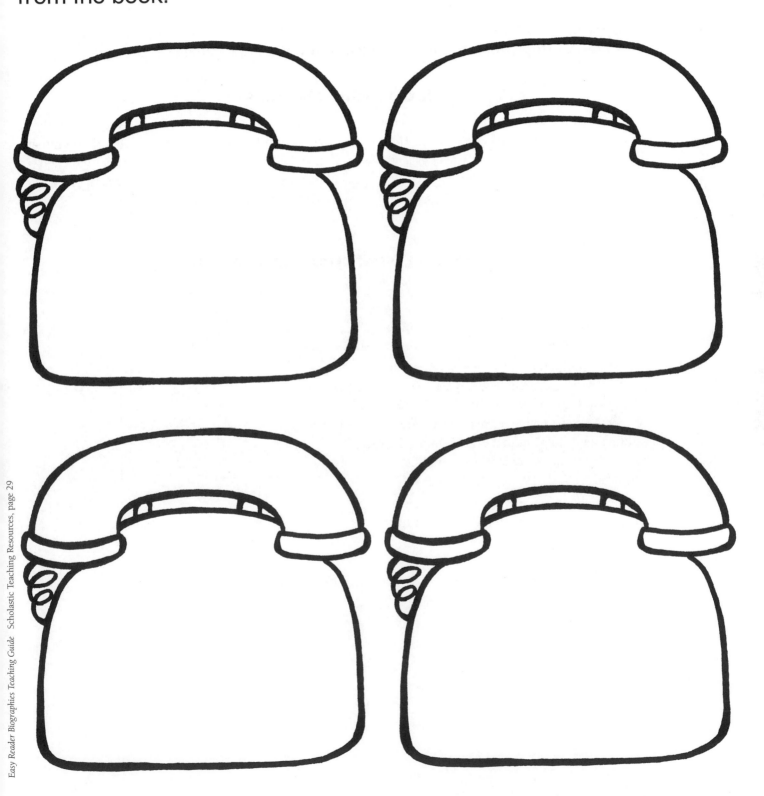

Cesar Chavez
A Leader for Change

Guided Reading Level: I

Word Count: 707

Average Words Per Page: 44

Spotlight Nonfiction Feature: List

Cesar Chavez (1927–1993) was a Mexican-American migrant farmworker. These workers had few rights. They worked long hours under terrible conditions and were paid very little. Cesar led the way to change by forming a union and encouraging farmworkers to vote. He also led boycotts and strikes. His efforts helped improve life for many migrant farmworkers and showed that people can make a difference by working together.

Introducing the Book

Begin a discussion about teamwork. Ask: *What are some jobs that are easier to do with a group? Have you ever worked with a team to help solve a problem? How did it feel to work together?*

Prepare children for reading by giving a background on workers' unions. Also explain the concepts of boycotts and strikes. Tell children that they will read about a man who led a union and planned boycotts and strikes in order to bring about important changes.

Spotlight Nonfiction Feature: List

Review with children that a common way to present nonfiction information is to give a main idea followed by several details that tell more about it. One way to do this is with a bulleted list.

Have children turn to page 8. Point out the sentences next to each bullet, explaining that each one gives a detail. Then ask: *Where is the main idea in this list?* Have a volunteer read the caption heading aloud. Explain that each item on the list will tell something more specific about the main idea.

Help children understand the list's purpose by turning it into a web on the board. In the center circle, write *How Life Was Hard for Migrant Farmworkers*. Then have children use the list to suggest ideas for the outer circles of the web (low pay, long hours, no rest, and so on).

Using the Reproducible

Distribute copies of the graphic organizer on page 31. Review with students how Cesar Chavez fought for change. Invite students to write four ways that Cesar worked to improve farmworkers' lives.

Book Links

For more information on Cesar Chavez, try these titles:

- *Cesar Chavez* by David Seidman (Scholastic, 2004)
- *Cesar Chavez* by Kitty Shea (Capstone, 2004)
- *Harvesting Hope: The Story of Cesar Chavez* by Kathleen Krull (Harcourt, 2003)

Signs of Change

Cesar Chavez helped change farmworkers' lives. In each sign,
write something he did that helped improve their lives.

Helen Keller
An Inspiring Life

Helen Keller (1880–1968) was born a healthy child. But at the age of two, tragedy struck: A severe illness left her both deaf and blind. She spent her early years frustrated and unable to communicate. But with perseverance and the help of teacher Annie Sullivan, Helen Keller grew up to be a highly educated and accomplished woman—showing the world that virtually any obstacle can be overcome.

Guided Reading Level: J

Word Count: 666

Average Words Per Page: 42

Spotlight Nonfiction Feature: Timeline

Introducing the Book

Invite children to talk about their personal heroes. What special things have these people accomplished? You might make a list on the board of qualities children admire in their heroes, such as bravery, perseverance, and hard work.

Tell children that today they will read about a person who could neither see nor hear. Explain that although she had many obstacles, this amazing woman overcame them all to reach her goals.

Spotlight Nonfiction Feature: Timeline

Tell children that many biographies are told in chronological order. Then explain that the events in a person's life can also be shown in a timeline. A timeline includes a short description of each event and tells when it happened.

Have children turn to pages 14–15. Tell children that most timelines have an introduction or caption—explain that they should read this first so they will know what the timeline will show them. Then ask: *What does the first point in the timeline show? Why do you think so?* (It shows the year Helen Keller was born; the timeline starts at the beginning of her life.)

Give children practice reading the timeline by asking questions such as: *How can you use the first two dates to figure out Helen's age at the time she got sick?* (Subtract 1880 from 1882; she was two years old.) *Why do two labels show the same year?* (Because two important events happened that year.) *Which event came first?* (Annie Sullivan's arrival came first.)

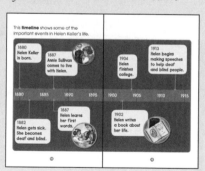

Using the Reproducible

Invite children to think about the many things Helen Keller accomplished during her lifetime. Distribute copies of the graphic organizer on page 33. Have students fill in each star with one of her accomplishments.

Book Links

For more information on Helen Keller, try these titles:

- *A Girl Named Helen Keller* by Margo Lundell (Scholastic, 1995)
- *A Picture Book of Helen Keller* by David A. Adler (Holiday House, 1991)
- *Helen Keller and the Big Storm* by Patricia Lakin (Simon & Schuster, 2002)

Shining Stars

Helen Keller accomplished many things in her life. In each star, write something she accomplished.

Martin Luther King, Jr.
A Man With a Dream

Guided Reading Level: I

Word Count: 707

Average Words Per Page: 44

Spotlight Nonfiction Feature: Illustrated Examples With Captions

Martin Luther King, Jr. (1929–1968), led the way to equality for all Americans. Growing up in Georgia, King suffered the effects of racism and segregation. He vowed that one day he would make our country a better place to live—and he did. With peaceful determination, Dr. King worked to make his dream come true.

Introducing the Book

Introduce the concept of peaceful problem solving by asking: *If you felt that a classmate was treating you unfairly, what could you do?* Lead children to see that people can stand up for their rights without fighting.

Explain that in some parts of our country, there were unfair laws for African Americans. Today they will read about a great man who helped solve this problem peacefully.

Spotlight Nonfiction Feature: Illustrated Examples With Captions

Review with children that a sentence that appears above, below, or beside a picture is called a *caption*. The picture helps readers visualize the information, and the caption tells readers what the picture shows.

Have children turn to pages 4–5. Explain that sometimes, one main idea can be shown with several different pictures. Read the heading at the top of page 4, pointing out that it tells the main idea. Next, have children point to each small picture and read the captions aloud. Emphasize that each picture and caption gives an example, or detail, about the main idea. Explain the signs

used in the third picture. Tell children that the word *colored* was used to refer to African Americans because of the color of their skin.

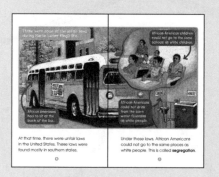

Using the Reproducible

Pass out copies of page 35 and talk about King's dreams for making America a better place. Ask: *What were some problems that he wanted to solve?* Next, ask children: *What dream do you have to make our country better?* Have children draw their face in the oval at the bottom of the page and then write about their own dream.

Book Links

For more information on Martin Luther King, Jr., try these titles:

- *Happy Birthday, Martin Luther King* by Jean Marzollo (Scholastic, 1993)
- *Martin's Big Words: The Life of Dr. Martin Luther King, Jr.* by Doreen Rappaport (Hyperion, 2001)
- *My Brother Martin: A Sister Remembers Growing Up With the Rev. Dr. Martin Luther King, Jr.* by Christine King Farris (Simon & Schuster, 2002)

Name _____ Date _____

American Dreams

Martin Luther King, Jr., had a dream to make America a better place for all people. Write about his dream in the first bubble. Then think about your own dream for America. Draw your face in the oval. Then write your dream in the second bubble.

Dr. King's Dream for America

My Dream for America

Abraham Lincoln
A Great President, a Great American

Abraham Lincoln lived from 1809 to 1865 and was president for the last four years of his life. Called "Honest Abe," this great American leader kept our country together with a victory in the Civil War, and helped to abolish slavery. From postmaster to lawyer to president, Abraham Lincoln was a man of determination.

Guided Reading Level: I

Word Count: 631

Average Words Per Page: 39

Spotlight Nonfiction Feature: Map

Introducing the Book

Ask: *What makes someone a great leader? What qualities should a leader have?* Begin a web on the board by writing *Leader* in the center circle. Invite children to suggest attributes, such as *honest, fair*, and *brave*, and write these words in surrounding circles.

Tell children that they will be reading about a very famous man who was an important leader many years ago: Abraham Lincoln. If children are familiar with this famous American, invite them to share any facts they know. Provide students with background information about the time period.

Spotlight Nonfiction Feature: Map

Discuss that a map shows what a place looks like from above. Explain that it's a flat picture of land on Earth viewed from above. Next, point out that there are many different kinds of maps. For instance, a physical map shows features like mountains and rivers. A political map shows borders of countries or states.

Turn to pages 10–11. First, read the main text. Then read the title and caption. Explain that the caption works like a map key—it tells what the colors on the map mean. Call on volunteers to read the names of the southern states. Ask: *What did these states want to do?* (They wanted to form

their own country.) Point out the compass rose in the corner and explain how to use it. Review what the letters *N, S, W*, and *E* stand for.

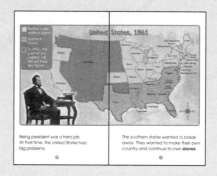

Using the Reproducible

Distribute page 37 and review with children that an *effect* is what happened and a *cause* is why it happened. Help children fill in the missing causes and effects. Lead them to see that Abraham Lincoln ran for president because people asked him to; that the Civil War started because the southern states attacked the northern states; and that the United States stayed together because Abraham Lincoln's army won.

Book Links

For more information on Abraham Lincoln, try these titles:

- *Abe Lincoln: The Boy Who Loved Books* by Kay Winters (Simon & Schuster, 2002)
- *Abe Lincoln's Hat* by Martha F. Brenner (Random House, 1994)
- *Mr. Lincoln's Whiskers* by Karen B. Winnick (Boyds Mills, 1996)

Cause and Effect

Read the causes and effects in the hats below. A cause is the reason something happened. An effect is the event that happened. Fill in the missing information.

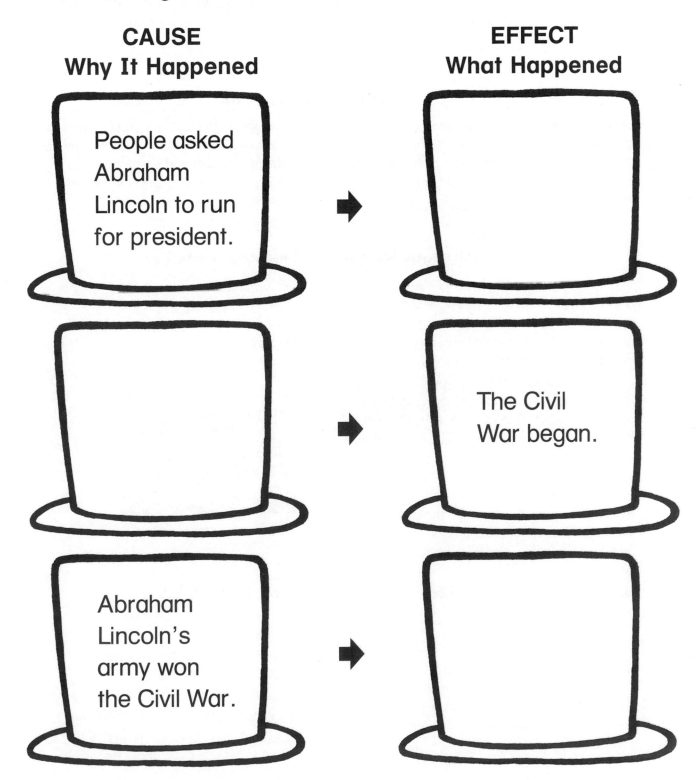

CAUSE
Why It Happened

EFFECT
What Happened

People asked Abraham Lincoln to run for president.

The Civil War began.

Abraham Lincoln's army won the Civil War.

Rosa Parks
Bus Ride to Freedom

Rosa Parks (1913–2005) is often called the "Mother of the Civil Rights Movement." Parks worked with the National Association for the Advancement of Colored People, but her defining moment came on a city bus in Alabama in 1955. When asked to give up her seat to a white passenger, she refused. Her arrest and trial led to the Montgomery Bus Boycott—and, eventually, to the end of segregation.

Guided Reading Level: J

Word Count: 826

Average Words Per Page: 52

Spotlight Nonfiction Feature: Timeline

Introducing the Book

Begin a discussion about the concept of fairness. Get children thinking with an example, such as: *If a teacher said that children with curly hair were not allowed to go to recess today, would that be fair? Why or why not?*

Explain that in some parts of our country, there were unfair laws for African Americans. Tell children they will read about an African-American woman who helped change these unfair laws by standing up for what she believed in.

Spotlight Nonfiction Feature: Timeline

Explain that a timeline shows a series of events and the order in which they happened. Timelines often show events that happened over long periods, so that readers can see at a glance how one event may have led to the next.

Have children turn to pages 14–15. Point out the timeline's introduction and have a volunteer read it aloud. Next, have children find the starting and ending dates. Ask: *How long a period can we see in this timeline?* (The timeline shows 92 years—the length of Rosa Parks's life.) Then have volunteers read the labels for each event. Make sure children read the events in sequential order, from left to right.

To assess comprehension, ask questions such as: *What happened first, the March on Washington or Rosa Parks's arrest? The events from 1955 and 1956 are very close together. How did one lead to the next?*

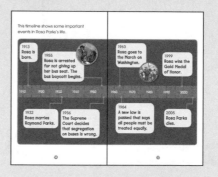

Using the Reproducible

Distribute copies of the reproducible on page 39. Ask: *In what ways were African Americans treated unfairly during Rosa Parks's life? What were the rules in restaurants and schools? What were the rules on the bus? How have those rules changed?* Invite children to look through the book for examples to complete the activity sheet.

Book Links

For more information on Rosa Parks, try these titles:

- *I Am Rosa Parks* by Rosa Parks with James Haskins (Dial, 1997)
- *If a Bus Could Talk: The Story of Rosa Parks* by Faith Ringgold (Simon & Schuster, 1999)
- *Rosa* by Nikki Giovanni (Henry Holt, 2005)

Then and Now

During Rosa Parks's life, there were unfair laws for African Americans. In each pair of buses, write about how the laws have changed. The first pair has been done for you.

THEN

African-American children could not go to the same schools as white children.

NOW

Everyone can go to the same schools.

THEN

NOW

THEN

NOW

Betsy Ross
The Story of Our Flag

Guided Reading Level: I

Word Count: 649

Average Words Per Page: 41

Spotlight Nonfiction Feature:
Diagram

Betsy Ross (1752–1836) is famous for the story of how the first American flag came to be. General George Washington, leader of the Colonial army, wanted a flag to signify the colonies' independence from England. No one knows for sure if Betsy Ross actually sewed the first flag, but the story is often told. It begins one day in 1776 when Washington asked Ross to sew a flag he had designed. But Ross had her own ideas—and so the famous design is sometimes called the "Betsy Ross flag."

Introducing the Book

Activate children's prior knowledge by asking what they know about our country's flag. Ask questions such as: *What colors are on the flag? What does the design look like? Where can you see our flag? What does it make you think of?*

Tell children that the American flag didn't always look the way it looks now. The first flag was made long ago, when our country was brand-new. Today they will hear a story of how the "Stars and Stripes" were born. Emphasize that we do not know if this story is actually true, but it is often told.

Spotlight Nonfiction Feature: Diagram

Discuss with children the definition of a diagram: a picture that helps readers understand information in a visual way. Diagrams can show what something looks like, what its parts look like, or how it works. Usually, diagrams have labels to help readers understand the picture.

Have children turn to pages 12–13 and ask a volunteer to read the titles above each diagram. Explain that the title tells what the diagram shows. Then have children read the call-out labels on each. Explain that these call-outs give more information about parts of the picture.

To assess comprehension, ask: *What information about the pictures do the labels give you?* (The labels tell the number of stars and stripes and what they stand for.)
How has the flag changed over the years? (The flag now has 50 stars.)

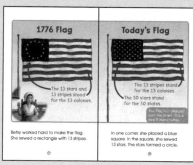

Using the Reproducible

Distribute copies of page 41 along with red, white, and blue crayons. Encourage children to use the illustration on page 12 for reference as they color their flags. Then have children read the topic in each box. They can look through the book to find the correct information.

Book Links

For more information on Betsy Ross and our nation's flag, try these titles:

- *Betsy Ross* by Alexandra Wallner (Holiday House, 1994)
- *Meet Our Flag, Old Glory* by April Jones Prince (Little, Brown, 2004)
- *Red, White and Blue: The Story of the American Flag* by John Herman (Penguin, 1998)

Betsy Ross's Flag

First, color the flag to look like the one Betsy Ross made. Then, write information from the story in each box.

Why we needed a flag:

Betsy's ideas for the flag:

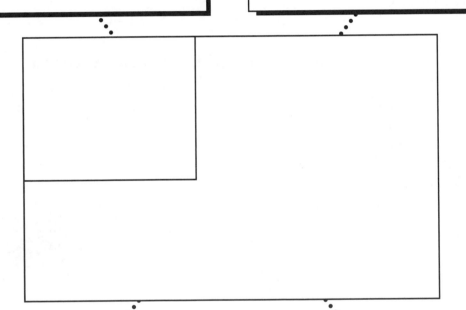

What the 13 stars and 13 stripes stand for:

How the flag looks different today:

Squanto
A Friend to the Pilgrims

Guided Reading Level: I

Word Count: 584

Average Words Per Page: 37

Spotlight Nonfiction Feature:
Diagram

Squanto, a Wampanoag, lived from about 1585 to 1622 in Patuxet—now known as Plymouth, Massachusetts. When the Pilgrims arrived in 1620, Squanto showed them how to hunt and plant crops. The Pilgrims had a bountiful harvest and shared a feast with Squanto and 90 Wampanoag. Today we commemorate this feast by celebrating Thanksgiving.

Introducing the Book

Build background by helping children make personal connections to Squanto's story. Ask: *If new students joined our class, what could you do to help them settle in? Would you tell them where materials are kept or give them other helpful advice about the classroom or school? What else could you do to make newcomers feel welcome?*

Explain to children that they will be reading about a Native American named Squanto. He welcomed the Pilgrims when they came to America by showing them how to survive in their new home. Explain that the United States was not yet a country.

Spotlight Nonfiction Feature: Diagram

Explain that a diagram is a kind of picture that shows the parts of something or how something works. Diagrams often have labels with arrows that connect to parts of the picture. Diagrams are useful because they help readers visualize the information they present.

Have children turn to the diagram on page 11. First, read the text at the bottom of the page. Next, read the caption and the diagram's labels. Have children trace the arrows' path from the labels to the diagram parts.

Ask: *What information do you get from the main text on this page?* (Corn, beans, and squash grow well together.) *What extra information does the diagram give you?* (The squash was planted a little apart from the other crops. The bean plants climbed the cornstalks.)

Using the Reproducible

Give children copies of the reproducible on page 43. Encourage them to pretend they are Pilgrims who received help from Squanto. Then invite them to write Squanto a thank-you note. Encourage children to use the idea bank for topics and include details they learned from the book. You might have them sign the letter with a typical Pilgrim's name, such as Humility or Resolved.

Book Links

For more information on Squanto, try these titles:

- *Giving Thanks: The 1621 Harvest Feast* by Kate Waters (Scholastic, 2001)
- *Squanto and the First Thanksgiving* by Eric Metaxas (Rabbit Ears Books, 1996)
- *Squanto's Journey: The Story of the First Thanksgiving* by Joseph Bruchac (Harcourt, 2000)

Name ______________________ Date ______________________

Thank You, Squanto

Imagine that you are a Pilgrim. Write a letter to Squanto thanking him for his help. You can use the idea bank to help you write.

Idea Bank

cold winter	hunting	great harvest
good teacher	catching fish	delicious feast
staying warm	planting crops	giving thanks

Dear Squanto,

____

____

____

____

____

____

Sincerely,

______________________,

a thankful Pilgrim

Harriet Tubman
Follow the North Star

Guided Reading Level: I

Word Count: 700

Average Words Per Page: 44

Spotlight Nonfiction Feature: Map

Harriet Tubman, who lived from about 1820 to 1913, was born a slave in Maryland. Tubman escaped to the North with help from the Underground Railroad, but she didn't stop there. She made the treacherous trip back and forth again and again, leading more than 300 slaves to freedom on the Underground Railroad—and never once losing a passenger.

Introducing the Book

Explain that long ago in our country, some people in the South had slaves. A slave was someone whom another person owned. Today no one is allowed to own another person. Back then, slaves had to do whatever their masters wanted. They were not free. They were not paid any money for their work, and they were treated poorly.

Help children understand how difficult life was for slaves. Ask: *Why is being free so important? How would you feel if you were not free?* Tell children that they will read about an incredibly brave woman who took risks not only to free herself but to help others escape, too.

Spotlight Nonfiction Feature: Map

Help children define what a map shows— a "bird's-eye view" of the world, or part of the world. Then introduce the term *transportation map.* Explain that this kind of map shows a route, or how one can travel, from one place to another.

Have children turn to the map on page 10. Point out the caption and have a volunteer read it aloud, explaining that it tells what route the map shows. Explain how to use the compass rose and what the letters stand for.

Have children find the beginning of the route, and ask: *Where did Harriet begin her trip?*

(Bucktown, Maryland) *In what direction did she travel?* (She traveled north.) Invite children to trace Harriet's route with a finger. When they reach the end of the line, ask: *Where did Harriet's route end?* (Philadelphia, Pennsylvania).

Using the Reproducible

Discuss what it may have been like to travel on the Underground Railroad. Ask: *How would you feel at the start of the trip? What are some dangerous things that could happen along the way? How would you feel when you reached the North?* Distribute page 45 and have children write a travel log about their route to freedom. At each "stop," they can write feelings and events. When they reach the star, they can write how it feels to be free.

Book Links

For more information on Harriet Tubman and the Underground Railroad, try these titles:

* *A Picture Book of Harriet Tubman* by David A. Adler (Holiday House, 1992)

* *If You Traveled on the Underground Railroad* by Ellen Levine (Scholastic, 1993)

* *Minty: A Story of Young Harriet Tubman* by Alan Schroeder (Dial, 1996)

Name _____   Date _____

My Path to Freedom

Imagine you are a passenger on the Underground Railroad. As you follow the path, write what happens and how you feel at each stop along the way. When you reach the last stop, write in the star how it feels to be free.

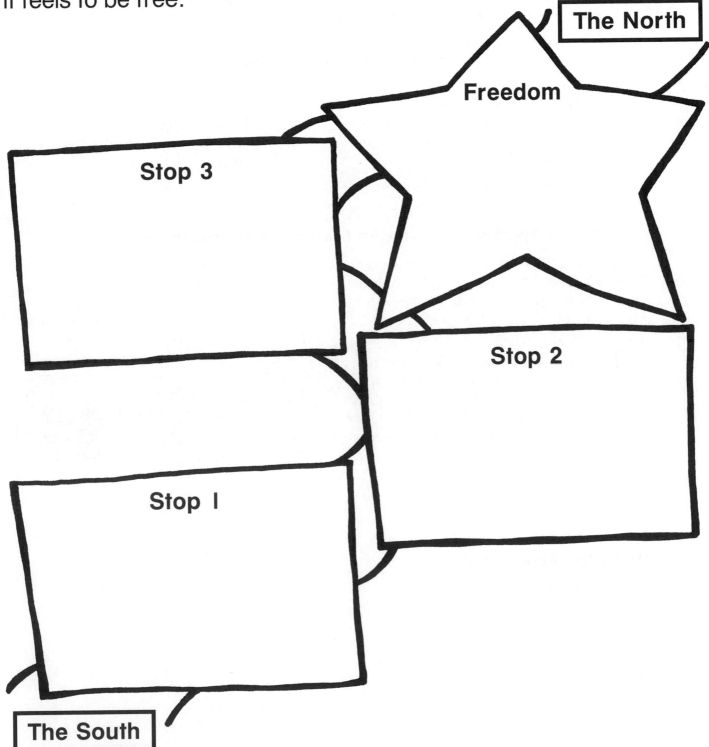

The North

Freedom

Stop 3

Stop 2

Stop 1

The South

George Washington
America's First President

Geoge Washington (1732–1799) is famous for being our country's first president. Born in Virginia, George Washington always had an interest in being a soldier. But when the American Revolutionary War broke out, he proved himself to be a natural leader. During the war, George Washington led the colonies to a stunning victory over England—and later, as president, united a new, independent nation.

Guided Reading Level: J

Word Count: 692

Average Words Per Page: 43

Spotlight Nonfiction Feature: List, Diagram

Introducing the Book

Invite children to tell what they know about the president of the United States. Ask: *What is the president's job?* Next, explain that long ago we did not have a president. In fact, the United States was not even a country!

Discuss that being president today is a very difficult and demanding job. But being our country's first president may have been even harder! Tell children that they will read about the man who helped form our nation and who became our first president.

Spotlight Nonfiction Features: List and Diagram

Explain that nonfiction text sometimes includes lists of facts. Before reading a list, children should read the heading to find out what the list is about. Have volunteers read aloud the heading and each point on page 7.

Remind children of another kind of list they may have seen: steps in a process. This type of list is often used for directions and includes words like *first*, *next*, and *last*. Ask: *Does the list on page 7 show steps in a process?* (No.) *How can you tell?* (Each fact takes place at the same time.) Lead children to see that the heading on page 7 gives the main idea and each fact provides a detail.

Next, explore the diagram on page 11. Explain that a diagram is a picture that can show the parts of something. It often has labels for each part. Point out that this diagram shows what George Washington wore on the day he became president. Invite children to read the labels aloud and trace the arrows to find each part of his outfit.

Using the Reproducible

Give children copies of page 47 and point out that the book tells the story of George Washington's life in sequence, or time order. Have children use information from the book to complete the event description in each box. Then invite them to trace the path with their fingers, reading the events in order that led up to George Washington's presidency.

Book Links 📖

For more information on George Washington, try these titles:

- *George Washington and the General's Dog* by Frank Murphy (Random House, 2002)
- *George Washington's Breakfast* by Jean Fritz (Coward McCann, 1969)
- *A Picture Book of George Washington* by David A. Adler (Holiday House, 1989)

Path to the Presidency

Many events happened in George Washington's life that led up to his presidency. Write the missing information in each box. Then read the events in order.

George was born in Virginia in the year

_____

When he was 16, George _____

_____

When George was 20, he _____

_____

During the Revolutionary War, George

_____

_____

Finally, in 1789, George Washington

_____

_____

Selected References

Boyton, A. & Blevins, W. (2005). *Nonfiction passages with graphic organizers for independent practice: Grades 2–4*. New York: Scholastic.

Boyton, A. & Blevins, W. (2004). *Teaching students to read nonfiction: Grades 2–4*. New York: Scholastic.

Kristo, J. V., & Bamford, R. A. (2004). *Nonfiction in focus: A comprehensive framework for helping students become independent readers and writers of nonfiction, K–6*. New York: Scholastic.

Susan B. Anthony

Parker, B. K. (1998). *Susan. B. Anthony: Daring to vote*. Brookfield, CT: Millbrook Press.

Ward, G. C. & Burns, K. (1999). *Not for ourselves alone: The story of Elizabeth Cady Stanton and Susan B. Anthony*. New York: Alfred A. Knopf.

Weisberg, B. (1988). *Susan. B. Anthony: Woman suffragist*. New York: Chelsea House.

Johnny Appleseed

Hodges, M. (1997). *The true tale of Johnny Appleseed*. New York: Holiday House.

Levine, E. (1986). *If you traveled west in a covered wagon*. New York: Scholastic.

Moore, E. (1964). *Johnny Appleseed*. New York: Scholastic.

Price, R. (1954). *Johnny Appleseed: Man and myth*. Urbana, OH: Urbana University.

Alexander Graham Bell

Haven, K. (2003). *Alexander Graham Bell: Inventor and visionary*. New York: Franklin Watts.

Time for Kids with Micklos, J. Jr. (2006). *Alexander Graham Bell: Inventor of the telephone*. New York: HarperCollins.

Webster, C. (2004). *Alexander Graham Bell and the telephone*. New York: Children's Press.

Cesar Chavez

Krull, K. (2003). *Harvesting hope: The story of Cesar Chavez*. San Diego: Harcourt.

McGregor, A. (2000). *Remembering Cesar: The legacy of Cesar Chavez*. Clovis, CA: Quill Driver Books.

Seidman, D. (2004). *Cesar Chavez: Labor leader*. New York: Franklin Watts.

Terzian, J. & Cramer, K. (1970). *Mighty hard road: The story of Cesar Chavez*. New York: Doubleday.

Helen Keller

Garrett, L. (2005). *Helen Keller: A photographic story of a life*. New York: DK.

Herrman, D. (1998). *Helen Keller: A life*. New York: Knopf.

Sullivan, G. (2000). *Helen Keller*. New York: Scholastic.

Martin Luther King, Jr.

de Kay, J. T. (1963). *Meet Martin Luther King, Jr.* New York: Random House.

Farris, C. K. (2003). *My brother Martin: A sister remembers growing up with the Rev. Dr. Martin Luther King, Jr.* New York: Simon & Schuster.

Jackson, G. (2001). *Martin Luther King, Jr.: A man of peace*. New York: Scholastic.

Abraham Lincoln

Freedman, R. (1987). *Lincoln: A photobiography*. New York: Clarion.

Marrin, A. (1997). *Commander in chief: Abraham Lincoln and the Civil War*. New York: Dutton.

McGovern. A. (1966). *If you grew up with Abraham Lincoln*. New York: Scholastic.

Stone, T. L. (2005). *Abraham Lincoln: A photographic story of a life*. New York: DK.

Rosa Parks

Adler, D. A. (1993). *A picture book of Rosa Parks*. New York: Holiday House.

Dubois, M. L. (2003). *Rosa Parks: A photo-illustrated biography*. Mankato: MN: Bridgestone Books.

McLeese, D. (2003). *Rosa Parks*. Vero Beach, FL: Rourke.

Parks, R. with Haskins, J. (1992). *Rosa Parks: My story*. New York: Puffin.

Weidt, M. N. (2003). *Rosa Parks*. Minneapolis: Lerner.

Betsy Ross

Duden, J. (2002). *Betsy Ross*. Mankato: MN: Bridgestone Books.

Frost, H. (2003). *Betsy Ross*. Mankato: MN: Pebble Books.

Miller, S. M. (2000). *Betsy Ross: American patriot*. New York: Chelsea House.

Wallner, A. (1994). *Betsy Ross*. New York: Holiday House.

Squanto

Black, S. W. (2002). *Let's read about Squanto*. New York: Scholastic.

Bruchac, J. (2000). *Squanto's journey: The story of the first Thanksgiving*. New York: Harcourt.

Grace, C. O. & Bruchac, M. M. with Plimoth Plantation (2001). *1621: A new look at Thanksgiving*. New York: Scholastic.

Kamma, A. (2001). *If you were at the first Thanksgiving*. New York: Scholastic.

Waters, K. in cooperation with Plimoth Plantation (2001). *Giving thanks: The 1621 harvest feast*. New York: Scholastic.

Harriet Tubman

Clinton, C. (2004). *Harriet Tubman: The road to freedom*. New York: Little, Brown.

McDonough, Y. Z. (2002). *Who was Harriet Tubman?* New York: Grosset & Dunlap.

McGovern, A. (1965). *"Wanted dead or alive" The true story of Harriet Tubman*. New York: Scholastic.

McMullan, K. (1991). *The story of Harriet Tubman, conductor of the Underground Railroad*. New York: Yearling.

Time for Kids with Skelton, R. (2005). *Harriet Tubman: A woman of courage*. New York: HarperCollins.

George Washington

Harness, C. (2000). *George Washington*. Washington, D.C.: National Geographic Society.

Hort, L. (2005). *George Washington: A photographic story of a life*. New York: DK.

January, B. (2003). *George Washington: Encyclopedia of the presidents*. New York: Children's Press.

Marrin, A. (2001). *George Washington and the founding of a nation*. New York: Dutton.